UNDERSTORY

Previous Winners of the Samuel French Morse Poetry Prize

*The Morse Poetry Prize*
*Edited by Guy Rotella*

MICHELLE BOISSEAU

# *Understory*

THE 1996 MORSE
POETRY PRIZE
❧ SELECTED AND
INTRODUCED BY
MOLLY PEACOCK

*Northeastern University Press*
BOSTON

Northeastern University Press

*Library of Congress Cataloging-in-Publication Data*
Boisseau, Michelle, 1955–
    Understory / Michelle Boisseau : selected and introduced by Molly Peacock.
      p.   cm.—(the 1996 Morse Poetry Prize)
     ISBN 1-55553-286-1 (pbk. : alk. paper)
     I. Peacock, Molly, 1947–  .  II. Title.   III. Series: Morse Poetry Prize ; 1996.
    PS3552.0555U53   1996
    811'.54—dc20          96-27940

Designed by Ann Twombly

Composed in Weiss by Graphic Composition, Athens, Georgia. Printed and bound by Thomson-Shore, Inc., Dexter, Michigan. The paper is Glatfelter Supple Opaque Recycled, an acid-free stock.

MANUFACTURED IN THE UNITED STATES OF AMERICA
00  99  98  97  96     5  4  3  2  1

*for Tom*
*the heart of every word*
*the soul of every sound*

It is like what we imagine knowledge to be:
dark, salt, clear, moving, utterly free,
drawn from the cold hard mouth
of the world, derived from the rocky breasts
forever, flowing and drawn, and since
our knowledge is historical, flowing, and flown.
— Elizabeth Bishop, "At the Fishhouses"


Nobody can tolerate crookneck squash being called turnips.
— Miroslav Holub, "On the Necessity of Truth"

ACKNOWLEDGMENTS

I would like to thank the editors of the following publications for
first publishing these poems, sometimes in another version:

| | |
|---|---|
| *Agni Review* | "Flesh Is Air, Too" |
| *Crazyhorse* | "Cold Harbor," "Family Formicidae," "Forerunner" |
| *Cream City Review* | "Likeness," "Gratia Plena," "Stillborn," "The Cry" |
| *Green Mountains Review* | "Black Mulberry," "Fog" |
| *Gettysburg Review* | "Cardinality" |
| *Indiana Review* | "Kindly Stopped," *"Sleeplessness:"* |
| *The Journal* | "Blood Sonata," "Auld Lang Syne" |
| *New Letters* | "—Cassiopeia at Noon," "Holler" |
| *North American Review* | "Pink Swing" |
| *Ohio Review* | "Pleiades" |
| *Ploughshares* | "The Next Child," "In Reserve," "Why You Said It" |
| *Southern Review* | "The Anatomy Theater at Padua," "Chalk Lineament" |

"The Cry" received the 1992 Lucille Medwick Award from the
Poetry Society of America.

"Against the Muse" appeared in *What Will Suffice: Contemporary
American Poets on the Art of Poetry,* ed. Christopher Buckley and
Christopher Merrill (Layton, Utah: Gibbs Smith, 1995).

"Multiflora" appeared in the chapbook *Some Will Tell You* (Louisville,
Ky.: White Fields Press, 1993).

This book was written with support from the National Endowment
for the Arts, the University of Missouri–Kansas City, the Kentucky
Arts Council, the Kentucky Foundation of Women, and Morehead
State University Research and Creative Productions Committee.

Deepest thanks to Tom Stroik, Susan Prospere, Mark Jarman, Andrew Hudgins, Nancy Eimers, and Bill Olsen. Thanks too to Rosellen Brown, Tracy Daugherty, and Mary Grimm for their abiding support.

# Contents

## III

# Introduction

Every poet must summon up courage of vision, but it takes a subtle kind of daring to underpin that vision, to supply its "understory." Michelle Boisseau, winner of the 1996 Samuel French Morse Prize for poetry, dares to display her vision *precisely*. In each poem she holds the focus of her spinning imagination until the exact, savory, morally unpredictable vocabulary comes firmly into place. Requiring precision from an energetic imagination means committing to ideas in all their complexity. So not only must Michelle Boisseau be fearless, she must be skilled—and she is. She delivers her poems with silken lines and such honesty of feeling and thought that one is hardly aware of how she is doing it. For all the talk about the form of a free verse poem coming from the internal pressure of the feeling and subject matter, that sort of seamlessness is really very rare, but I found it here—consistently.

Conveying a palpable sense of the understory of experience allows Boisseau to risk what might, with less intelligence and directness, be pedestrian subject matter for a woman. Her book begins with poems about motherhood. *Ho hum*, you may think as you resist being drawn in to yet another backyard with yet another swingset. To such a spot is exactly where you will be led, but not for a story of motherly fortitude. Boisseau goes for the multi-story of a highly contemporary family, one with a stepdaughter and a daughter, one with a husband and wife with their own past histories. In "Pink Swing" she designs a rhythmic musculature that almost flexes one image into the next:

> Disc of pink plastic dangling
> from the rope, monkey swing we hung
> last August for her visit. The thinnest breeze

pushes it above the grassless spot. Pendent
from the branch that lets it swing
but keeps it tethered, all it can do

is describe its small territory
in squiggles and arcs, to jerk and dance
at the end of its line, as if trying
to escape, to slip the rope and fly off
even if just to plummet like a waterlogged
star into the hedges. How awful is childhood—

the child only potential on a rope.

By animating the swing Boisseau propels an idea onto the page—an
emotional struggle, and the struggle for growth—which she explores
and re-explores.

Personal poets often long to extend private life into the world
at large, and few are able to. The common phrase for this is "going
beyond" the personal. What is fascinating about the development of
*Understory* is that the poet does bring her powers to bear on the world
outside the immediate neighborhood of the self, but she does so
through her determination to go into—under—the personal, dis-
covering there the roots of larger societal situations. Part I of *Un-
derstory* concentrates on the intensely intimate experiences of the
young family; the second part extends to the social environment of
this family (with a particularly arresting poem about the aftermath
of an Easter dinner in "Chalk Lineament," where a child draws the
outline of her grandfather spread-eagled on the driveway); and the
third brings the poet and her themes into contact with the politi-
cal—and historical—world.

Throughout her poems Boisseau shows a willingness to conjec-
ture, to ask questions and to answer them complexly or with qualifi-
cations. It surprises me to call so casual and visual a book learned as
well, but so it is. Quotations and references relax into the imaginative
flow: Dunsinane with a child running around a breakfast table, a
"bearded physician scooping" a "baby out into the damp room" ironi-

cally followed by a quotation from Pliny. We hear the likes of George Herbert, Aristotle, and Voltaire, the canon of a Catholic girlhood brought to the breakfast room, or, in the last section, to the "strange orange/rhombus of a Eurostyle room" in Ghent, where the speaker is "glued to CNN updates, . . . waiting for the last/US hostage, Terry Anderson, to step/onto the hospital balcony."

The task of selecting a winner from among the ten excellent manuscripts forwarded to me as final judge of this year's prize was particularly gruesome; each finalist certainly deserves publication. To distinguish among the exciting variety of styles and voices, I decided I must set as my standard a consistent combination of passion and virtuosity, not only in the star poems that flare across a manuscript, but in the entire constellation of the manuscript's poems. In setting that standard, I set my heart on an eloquent universe, and found the poems of *Understory*. With sensuous wordplay Boisseau shows how metaphor underpins—under*stands*—the world. "And even the mundane/pickup truck has a *bed*/to carry kindling," she writes in "Likeness." "Metaphor hitches the impossible/to the passable, the wonder/ to the wanderer," the poet continues, asking, "What's the use of metaphor if it can't make loss/fathomable, and the loss of loss:/a fathom is the measure of the arms/outstretched." So she makes poetry the experience of experience.

MOLLY PEACOCK

I

# Black Mulberry

Spindly sucker of the soil, lifting
a whole pond into its crown, the mulberry
stains the fence's whitewash
luscious and pelts us with fine purple
tones, notes not yet bundled into music.
I hold my daughter on my hip and tug
a branch down to us. A pluck
and it arcs away, more notes bouncing
off our heads. Berry in my fingers,
over her lips just to watch her squint
and pucker. I like to believe
experience can come this way, hand
to mouth and a minute explosion
follows on the tongue, like a word.
This is leaf and this and this.
This transparency, stuff
you can touch but hardly grasp, is water—
on the windows, muttering into the bathtub,
and far down in the yellow plastic cup.
Cinnamon, cloves, tarragon, pepper
I lift from the shelf for her to sniff:
What is it? What do you want from me?
All those months we answered each other
like those two who loved separated by a wall,
with her on that side knocking,
and me knocking back on this,
and the wall itself. I'd ease myself
behind the steering wheel, slide
in a cassette and drive hours through the hills
with Puccini pouring over us—
*Oh, dolci baci, o languide carezze*—
just to feel her tumbling inside me
like hunger, feel her brute music

inside the music, humming
back to me through the blood.
Pyramus, Thisbe, and the mulberry,
the old story of blood and natural sympathy.
The white berries went dark
in an instant, for the dead lovers
had soaked the earth through—
as if the recompense for sorrow
echoed in the trees, a narcissus
beside a puddle, a bracelet of stars,
fall and winter shriveled by a mother's loss.
It's the way I fool myself. Even when
we were close as rain and root,
and I could feel her head pressing
against the sky, it wasn't me she answered
so much as a farther rumbling,
some necessity already out of my hands.

# Pink Swing

## 1.

I play architect to my stepdaughter's heart,
drawing a house to her heart's desire:
"That's your and daddy's room. Now make a red one

for me. Now one for mommy." (I comply, I comply.
If this is a test, I will pass it.)
"Now a little house for the cat,

and put the pink swing in the tree."
When I've finished—making sure every door
has a knob, each window a curtain—

she spreads the picture on the floor and sings to it.
She has us where she wants us, under one
newshingled roof, and means to make us happy.

## 2.

Months after she's gone back, we're still finding her:
a bouquet of crayons under sofa cushions,
green spool of a Tinkertoy, farmyard ladder
the length of a pencil. This side of custody,
our affections go in safekeeping.

Give up the yellow anklet you found
clinging to the sheets. With each thing
we drop in a shoe box—wooden chicken, scuffed
baby that fits in the pocket—we find we're singing
the song she taught us: "Oh, where have you been

Billy Boy, Billy Boy? Oh, where
have you . . . ?" Her voice darts
around our heads like a dragonfly
on a thread, a bead of mercury rolling
inside a bottle given a feverish child.

3.

Before you punch the eleven numbers
that call your daughter up, you take a deep breath

and swing yourself into thin air. What can you say
to a small child through a telephone?

What of yourself can you push through a thousand
miles of switches that she might catch?

She's too young to listen long, one ear to your voice seeping
from the housing, the other taking in

the clatter of her mother listening from another room.
When you say, "Katie, the cat is sleeping

in the flowers, they want you to pick them,"
how can she believe you? She can see for herself

it's starting to snow again, a shaggy sleet
that ticks like static against the window.

4.

Flutter kicking up our legs to make room
for herself, one morning she jumped
into bed with us and said, "Hey guys,
I'm back!" as if sleep were a place
night carried her, milkweed

fluff lofted through the dream trees.
Waking up these days, where does she imagine you?
The polka dot that shrank
into the road the morning she hopped
from foot to foot in the parking lot?

Is the world to her smooth
as a cartoon, one seamless surface
then the door pops open
with you in it? You're thrown back
on yourself at age four, fishing inside
the great box of flimsy clues.

But the smell of graham crackers, the stiffness
of church shoes, don't reveal her
and they can't convince you
she knows you're coming back.

5.

Disc of pink plastic dangling
from the rope, monkey swing we hung
last August for her visit. The thinnest breeze
pushes it above the grassless spot. Pendent
from the branch that lets it swing
but keeps it tethered, all it can do

is describe its small territory
in squiggles and arcs, to jerk and dance
at the end of its line, as if trying
to escape, to slip the rope and fly off
even if just to plummet like a waterlogged
star into the hedges. How awful is childhood—

the child only potential on a rope. When it rains,
the water runs from her. When it snows,
she wears a skirt of it. And every blessed minute
there's a chittering in the broad sky
that seems to mean something,
a something that means to exclude her.

## Gratia Plena

I didn't feel a spark, a dandelion
exploding in seed, a new planet.
And I was far from Fra Angelico,
Simone Martini—those old masters
who always left a cool vessel and spray
of lilies to catch the shooting soul:
Ave, Maria! and in through the window
rolls Gabriel in gold leaf. Gratia plena!
and the pale girl's hands fly up
as if to bat away the spidery star
lofted toward her. Remember when the happy
shuffling of chromosomes began?
My face in your shoulder, your mouth
against my ear, how we were trying
to keep quiet while the whole household
conspired to muffle us: your brother
in the kitchen clanking pots for supper,
Katie and her cousins banging away
on the upright piano and the guinea pig
beside the guest bed squeaking
from her cedar-chip cavern. We tried
to keep quiet until we forgot ourselves,
the blazing pavilions for our own
Virginia reel, and we tumbled down warm
dunes to breakers that flung phosphorescent
nets about us. Lying back afterwards
face to face in the froth of sheets, we watched
the skiff we launched cross the horizon
toward the still rattling household.

## Family Formicidae

Around her arms captured ants
streak like wire bracelets. Through the grass
and over the blacktop my stepdaughter
chases the elusive ones and delivers
them to the withered jungle
in a mayonnaise jar.

*If I don't hurry they'll burn*
*their pinprick feet*

She hardly stops while I can barely start.
Eight months along, I've slung myself
in the porch swing, rockabye, rockabye
all afternoon lolled by the urgency
of this other one stretching inside me.
Now and then Katie will bend over me
and magisterially pat my broad belly.
This summer when we picked her up
she closed a doll in her shirt
and nursed it all the way
from Wisconsin. Now she's moved on
to livelier stories—entire clans swept
toward the totable heaven I hold on my knees.

*Go in there, in with your dead friends,*
*your crippled friends*
*and your really really live friends*

It's not revenge exactly
which is never exact. It's that the sputtering
wasp covets her clover tiara.
The longtail skipper is laughing
in the gladiolus juice. She assigns motive
to the foamflower, scolds a roof
of johnson grass for its flimsy design

and shames the pill bugs,
such dull armor. Come dark, the brilliant families
rising from the lawn will be taken
for their floating slowness.

*In this fist a fast fellow,*
*in this a biter who's so mad at me*

What would a god of insects be
but small and stern and resolute?
Clattering across the porch, she swoops
in with another pair of soldiers
(yes, she's saved some for the peonies).
Since she's a god, I'm another—
swollen, inattentive, last
audience for a minuscule soul.
I offer my belly to her handspan, letting her
take her measure of how this other
jumps against her fingers,
of how close the end must be.

# Multiflora

On every branch a bird, a bug
on every blade, a whistle, shriek, hum
from every breath of space.

Too many trees here smeared with moss,
too many green thoughts. My smallest
movement is a grand maneuver.

I have been pregnant so long
even my feet don't know me. They haul
their shadows beneath the porch swing

like overladen wagons.
        Wild rose, multiflora
pouring from the hedges, through the forest

understory, into cornfields, pastures, spooling
the battered legs of the picnic table,
nudging the kitchen threshold, you puff and blur

our blueprints, our combed sectors, our deeds.
All the loving hands turn upward:
take me, take me.

# Blood Sonata

Plump envelope, baby
folded twice in flannel,
tucked into a glass box
(though she won't wait for kisses
to wake her), and wheeled in
to us, the nurse's crepe soles
lightly smacking the polished floor.
The bed sits me up and you
lift her to me and settle her
above the incision. Unwrap the crystal
flutes you've brought from home
and let's knock them into music
as you kick your shoes off
and scoot in beside me.
\*   \*   \*

And if she bear a maid child,
then she shall be unclean
two weeks . . . and whosoever toucheth
her bed shall wash his clothes
and bathe himself
and be unclean until the evening . . .
and if any man lie
with her at all
and her flowers
be upon him he shall be unclean
for seven days and all
the bed whereon
he lieth shall be unclean.
—Leviticus
\*   \*   \*

On the operating table they curtained
me off from myself and I played along,
pretending to be blinded while I watched
them work in the silver hood
of the hanging lamp, a little window
to my body. The surgeon's hand
crossed my belly and presto,
a widening smile of blood the nurse
patted with gauze. Then the hood
was shifted, the anesthetics
coiled in my head and I saw only
a white corner of the room, an envelope flap,
until the pediatrician appeared with her,
blue, gluey, and blinking.
\*   \*   \*
The female is
as it were
a deformed male.
—Aristotle
\*   \*   \*
No wonder the riddle tripped them up:
Not of woman born. Not of woman
as in not borne through
the narrow canal? The bearded
physician scooping the baby out
steaming into the damp room.
Faces flickering by the peat fire,
the hushed women dabbed the blood and gel
from the soft head, the toes. Only afterwards
do they turn to the one laid out
on the plank table (not of woman
born, for woman no longer?)
and tuck her back inside herself, wind her body
like a spindle in fresh linen.
\*   \*   \*

Contact with it turns
new wine sour, crops touched
by it become barren, grafts
die, seeds in gardens
are dried up, the fruit
of the trees falls off,
the bright surface of mirrors
in which it is merely reflected
are dimmed, the edge of steel,
and the gleam of ivory
are dulled, the hives of bees
die, even bronze and iron
are at once seized by rust.
—Pliny the Elder
*   *   *
Where's the shame for it?
A shame instead to flush away
this bright excess flowing
from me without first stopping
to steady myself against the dizzy tiles
and admire the red tethers tumbling
through the watery world, the blood
pooling at the bottom like a dropped robe.
Wet plums in a white bowl
and I the orchard. How could I feel shame
in the fact of it? as the sky's
a blue fact stretched tight as silk
above the hospital and the green facts
of pines pouring down the hillsides.

# Fog

Here begin dreams of flight, the wallpaper
coasting past with the watery plains
of woodwork, the terrain of rug beneath you

like a gone planet. Here the land
of giants begins, our hands a waterfall
of touch, our bodies looming in fog

the trees launch into the nursery windows.
Licking at our heels, the fog follows us
down the stairs, sallies through the screen door

then rolls into the creek like a hedgehog.
5 a.m., you're flying in our arms,
your gaze fixed on the architecture

that is face, stanchion and roof,
portals you stare into: What are you?
Where have you come from?

—while all about us float the gritty
sands of dawn, a flecked light
like wild rice drifting in a pot,

nothing more and nothing less, and the work
of sorting it out—light and dark,
first and last. But the only baptism

we can give you is hardly ours
to give, the fog loosed from the hillsides
and dampening the whole still house.

## The Cry

I hear it accelerate
in the pickup truck, dragging a banner
of tunes through the slow afternoon.
I hear it in the fabric shaken
through the trees, lawnmower and birdsong:
here, here, here I am.
I go to check, but you haven't stirred.
A great small weight
at standstill, hurled
against the mattress, breathing, breathing.
What steady work it is
for you to live.
What steady work it is to give
you what you cry for.

And what does it mean?
Mother. *Parent* falls lightly
across the shoulders, the skin
soaking up the fragrance
of cut grass. But *Mother*
is a heavy necklace, silver filaments
weighted with lead sinkers. Heavier.
A stone yoke to drag the cart
of history behind us.

Enough of that—it's the real cry now
hoisting me up the stairs,
one end of it hooked
to my sternum, fish
on a line, piano on a pulley.
So these are the heartstrings,
pulled by a river of sound
and eased (the smell of you breaks

through my rib cage like light)
as the cry is satisfied.

Are these the claims for Mother:
soothe, food, please, whatever
is smooth as the flesh
cut open, the pear-shaped
womb, the avocado
and its child in a slick brown coat?

Back you go.
Into your safe cage.
As my mother gave me, I give
to you, daughter, already
some harm, some shudder at the sound.

# Cardinality

It's a party trick the baby performs
as she wobbles through the kitchen

from one pair of legs to another,
a benevolent forest sprung up

for her pleasure. Count on your fingers,
we tell her. And as she's watched us,

she plucks from her fist the forefinger,
then middle finger, her hands fidgety wings.

One two, she says. Our friends laugh
and tip back their beers. Sure, she can't count yet,

but she likes the game along with the chant
that separates one thing from another,

the marching alarm clock she totes through the house,
the eight nesting cups she heaves overhead.

Besides, laughing people are bound
to pick her up, ride her around on a hip,

give her a taste of peppers drizzled with sesame,
a sip of startling tonic. Later as she ponders

bathwater dripping off her fingers, I look up
from a magazine's gray page and she's at it again

—one, two—the thrill of sequence
launched from her hands, of choosing which

to watch for: the drop budding from her finger,
the blink of it in the air, or the quick

dint that closes just as she sees it.
I know it's a weakness to figure choice

into her task. Long ago the key was turned,
the ticking set in motion. It's the simplest of stories,

about how we get here and get pushed in turn.
The child's round head pushes its one, one, one

into the world and then the lament begins
about being set apart, about being next in line.

## Forerunner

*White is their color and behold my head.*
      —George Herbert

Like a spigot some dream is shut off
and I'm awake in the dead center
of the night that stops to let me off.
It hulks in the doorway,
this angel stinking of wet cement
and ashes. I sit up and listen
down the hall if it's hurt the baby.
She whimpers once then sinks in milksleep.

Was it looking in the window
when I touched the four walls
of the nursery and checked the locks
and covered her up again, afghan,
blanket of knots? I can make out
the snarled mat of its wings,
wet and swollen with the cloudy stories
it fell through: too heavy to lift
beyond the threshold, or let it turn around
and go back the way it came.

Before bed I carried her onto the porch,
then farther onto the cool road
and the bridge where the creek whisks
its silver clothes over the stones.
Was it perched in the tree filaments
to notice her, curled anchor
against the gloam of my nightgown, her eyes
wide to the splinters of stars?

The croak of peepers in their slick closets
filled the air and the sky lit

the tips of her hair. But for the slight
heft of her, I felt a featherweight too,
light enough to drift into those cirrus—
but I didn't admit it, since it's bad luck
to admit such happiness.

Brigantine in a bottle, it's cramped
in the doorframe and quiet
as a mirror looking at itself.
If I said, What do you want with her?
if I climbed out to touch the grease
shining on its feathers, there'd be nothing
to put my hand to, vane or shaft
tapered to the invisible end.

II

## —Cassiopeia at Noon

The gaze is no longer leveled
at me. Just another aspect
of landscape, I am round and bluff
as the antediluvian hills
across the lake, anonymous
as this water maple, our compass
of shade and dry towels.

Now I see how I have hurried
from doorway to doorway
like someone caught in a downpour.
Since I was 12 it was duck and cover,
Chica, Chica, Catholic girl
hugging books across her chest.
Under surveillance.

It's easy here in obscurity,
room to stretch my sand-smeared legs,
let my suit gape where it will,
unwind the generic gray hairs
like roads out of town:
so long, so long.
Soon, I shall be invisible—

# Why You Said It

*for my sister Madeline*

Then you've forgotten how we couldn't wait
for the bulldozers to raze that house
on Ridge Road. At the fresh edge
they'd butted into the woods,
the machines sat stalled for days, reluctant
to finish up the job. The goldfish pond
had already dried down to its beer cans
when our brothers started it, a few stones
to break the monotony of a picture window.
The provocation of the little flaws.
Kites of glass crunched under our feet
as we thumped through the empty rooms
like dice in a shoe box. The wallpaper
of smug begonias, one yank and it flowed
up the walls in long satisfying strips.
Wrapping ourselves in those paper boas,
we yelled, Goodbye, Good riddance,
Hit the road, Jack! and slammed the doors
harder, harder so cakes of plaster
slid through our hair. For an hour we rode
the bannister but couldn't bear how it
shuddered under our weight—
trying to make the best of things—
so we kicked it down the stairs.
And don't you remember the crowning touch?
We lassoed the chandelier with a scrounged necktie
and brought it down like a house of ice.

See how far back it goes. It's the tooth
I couldn't stop worrying till the roots
popped in my gums, the puncture in the cloth

that let you tear the lavender dress
into a cloud of lint. Once something starts
toward ruin, how good it feels
to help it go. That's why last night
when your lover hoisted his head
above yours—his scapegrace grin
a diffident shirt glimpsed above battlements—
something teetered in the balance,
scales in such airy equipoise
you couldn't help but tip them with a word.

## In Reserve

Your husband's laugh, a glass of grenadine.
          You greet the guests, steer coats onto your arms.
Ice rattles the kitchen: he's mixing drinks.

          You stand where you can keep an eye on him.
A glance from you, your face cool rising cream,
          and I know whatever I might say—vague

murmurings in one of the kid's tidy rooms
          so you might open up—would be betrayal.
I compose myself. I'll not notice you

          notice already he has fixed the evening
on someone's out-of-town sister, neutral
          lovely blond. Over her shoulder a green

scarf drifts like a bright apology he touches.
          —*I like this material.* —*Are you sure*
*I'm not keeping you from your other guests?*

          We'll all be drunk soon. Walk softly where starlings
have settled down in trees. They will wake
to one pebble, the back door's silver click.

## Pleiades

Fleet in the sky, but on earth,
though no one mentions it, we were heavy-footed.
That's the way with the daughters
of someone who grunts under the weight
of it all. I dragged my feet the most:
single file through the fields,
the end of the line was my place,
easy pickings. From his spot in the thicket
he was soft, a fingertip poking
from a frayed glove. His belt gleamed
like molasses. Of course, we were proud
of our likeness, seven mirrors
trampling the yellow grasses.
Naturally we fascinated him,
fastened him to us the way goldfish
catch a cat, swish and flicker
in the reflecting pond. To get close
is only to get wet in what heals
right back up again, the seven seas
poured into a single basin.

As my sisters shrank from sight,
my lungs started aching—I'd gone so deep
from them into the hushed woods,
the ferns rocking after me
like a restless bed. Beneath a curl
of hair his earring flashed
in the leaves, a moon
hollowed out. Flecks of limestone
dusted his beard and lips.
Sit here. He made a throne
of his lap. And I did what he said.

Do you suppose words are easy boats,
deep-hulled, creaking with wheat
and bumping against the morning docks?
Overnight the harbor silted up.
When I opened my mouth to tell
it filled with sand, a thousand
starlings erupted from a tree.
My sisters hardly suspected
except I grew so dim, a penny
snuffed under falling sands.
You there, feet soaked with dew,
your neck aching because you've looked up
so long, I am the dark one,
the seventh in the cluster of six,
the one you can't see
since they've hidden me
inside this glowing knot.

# The Anatomy Theater at Padua

title page, *De Humani Corporis Fabrica*, 1547

As there's no malice in science, there's nothing
personal about this rowdy crowd. One student
brought in a dancing dog, another a monkey
who spills orange rind on the men's velvet feet.
Such a horde of jubilation you'd think

the opened body had released them
like that minor god and his sack of pent up winds.
In the etching's center a skeleton rides
a railing. One jostled boy peers through
the low spy holes of the pelvis:

guess who? guess who? a barn owl
whirring in a hollow tree. Amid the scholars
down on stage, their beards hanging
like spades above their robes, the author
Andreus Vesalius illustrates the true

method of dissection, the fabric
of the human body. The corpse's skin
folds back neatly on louvered doors,
showing the crowded room
we each are, the perfect fit.

But who could you be? Some poor soul
dragged from the steaming hill beyond the city gates?

Your face is turned aside as if in modesty.
You're the only one naked among them,
a woman. I see now the artist's attention
to shading, the scratches on the copper plate
that indicate the rise of breasts, the dark nipples.

And this blur is your flowery uterus.
Shoulder to shoulder they hover above the opened
place the way men gather to dip
their dippers in a rain barrel or call
into a well where someone has fallen in.

## *Against the Muse*

Go down to the stream and dip your rosebud
      fingernails among the fish flickering
          like earrings in a roomful
of dancers, go down to that stream,
those neoclassical waters
            where the humming of houseboys
    beating laundry with willow sticks
       frames you like a really good haircut,
go down to that stream, take your gold
sandals with you and leave my rivers alone.

        I don't know what these slumped roofs
along the banks are,
       just the way I like it,
    so discouraged-looking at first I can't tell
if they're abandoned barns or apartment houses,
the yellow kitchen clock, the strip of garden
        with a view of the 5:08 and the 10:40
      that hardly come around anymore,
and the barges unbraiding the muddy water
     rattle with coal raked out of my head.

I'm tired of them always inviting you
        as soon as a basket appears
    without a load of apricots
or canaries. Even if they slapped you together
       with creek mud instead of blue foam
         and took some plastic drinking straws
           instead of reeds to blow you up,
    they'd still dress you in wafting stuff
       so all the black ties and the bartender
out on the terrace would turn to see the wonder.
    A little breeze comes up and your frock
laps about you, fine feathers

                    though no bones to speak of,
wren, sparrow,

                    and hardly the nerve
to move out of earshot, turn your back
on the great house,
                    window dazzle, banked blossoms,
                    Euclidean inclinations,
                    and come down here where the moss
        can give you a good soaking and,
            if you hear them coming for you,
fill you with its messages.

## Sleeplessness:

These sibilants aren't the right sound
for it, nor the loosening sonorants

of *insomnia*. The body
doesn't relinquish the day, hissing

as it gives itself over, breath
by deeper breath. Though you wander

the weird factory for hours,
you don't get lost, drop off somewhere

so you can find yourself at dawn
floating back into your bed

like a scarf. Without sleep, morning
is no surprise. You've watched it assemble,

the day already old when you kick
the blanket off. You're the same except

giving the drapery a jerk, how skittery you are.
Awake all night means, once again,

you left everything wide open.
Look around your feet. Marbles clacking

in a box, the room has filled with grackles.
Their tin feet scritch across the floor.

Because you would not sleep, you asked for it.
They fix you with yellow eyes.

Their whir and chack make sense to you.

## Kindly Stopped

Mid-October rain brought down all the leaves.
Cold-plastered to the patio,
dull citizens for this season—
they hardly had the chance to change.

This fall, it's ten years
since your death. The second husband
you never had, the children,
the kitchen strung with copper pots—

you won't forgive any of us.
Dickinson resurrected *kindly*,
an archaic choice, to remind us
that beyond gentleness lies nature

and the nature of death is to stop for us.
Why do I bother? The play of words
no longer attracts you, shrunk like a mole
in the nest of them, the looped knots and roots.

In my new house I expected a few weeks
of living inside a genial dome of leaves.
Now that they've fallen, there you are, strident,
where the silver maples were picked clean.

# Auld Lang Syne

*The dead center is always hardened and sometimes*
*both centers are hardened.*
—Machine Shop Work, *1942 technical manual*

In the Kubota dealer's gravel lot
across the road, two ramrod men wander
all morning inspecting the tractor cabs,

kicking the harrows no one ever buys,
pretending imagination hasn't failed them
like the rest of us. Even this weather

vacillates, a solid week of ice clicking
on the roof, lacquering the house shut,
the kitchen's ornamental cherry. Rain

or snow it can't muster. At breakfast
since nothing's new, we tease the kids,
Aren't you starved? You haven't eaten

since last year! And we go on poking
each other through TV bowl games and naps
and the early dark: I haven't had a drink

all year. We haven't had sex since—
The baby waves a fist of bread
at the slop, loose solder sizzling

in the mud, this winter pulled down
like a wet hat on our heads.
How can we look forward when we can't see

fifty yards without running up against
a monotony of trees, a hill clabbered
with leaves and crumbling limbwrack,

the narrow road writhing past.
We know full well our neighbor
leveled his lot to accommodate a wealth

of orange machinery, but we pretend
he cut it like a cake as punishment
for dropping night on us in the afternoon,

for settling for less. Everybody knows
how the woods dissemble, but those others—
the Florentine with his chain of rhymes,

the brother and sister and their thread
of crumbs—they at least found a directive
to abandon hope or a bold candy house

to break apart and suck. We've lived here
too long to be tricked into promising
this year will be different:

we will, we won't, not again this year,
this town of dismal churches and barbers,
a supermarket where overcoats mumble

at black bananas and the pictures
on canned corn, canned pears, crisco.
The baby's complaint is as good as any.

B-b-b, she says, struggling to name
this flavor in the house, the trees, this mood
parked at our dinner table like the salt.

## The Next Child

I tell you she was here again last night.
While the wind scratched at the rafters
and we were fumbling around
the nightstand for diaphragm and jelly,
while Anna was giving her report from sleep,
rolling the heavy words through her crib slats
like cannonballs—our next child,
the child we will not have, rode in again,
rode in on the rain. Once again the chimney cap
was prized off and now lies pitched
in my newly bedded impatiens.
Again the tick tick in the fireplace,
the house filling with a reeking
grey muffle. And something fluttered
into the dogwood, its dark ribs bursting
the milkstars I'd set my sights on
into a thousand brown planets.
Brown planets? See what's happened to me?
When I look at the sky the sun
winks its swords at me. The telltale glint
through the trees mesmerized
the besieged at Dunsinane.
I don't know what it is, but it's not sky blue.

Anna races herself around and around
the breakfast table as if she could
catch herself coming and going.
Enough already, we tell her, such hunger
turned the tigers to a streak of butter
littered with parasols and purple shoes.
We've scattered this morning's paper
with the broken globes of oranges.
I twist a shard into the sunlight

to show her how it erupts, golden,
an atmosphere that flares brief as history,
then rains down sticky on our heads.
But even this bitter rind would be sweet
to that other child, snugged in the attic.
Light as fiberglass, she hangs by her feet
like a shut umbrella.

# Stillborn

Little fisted face in the unbearable coffin,
drifting inside the nest of satin, milk
whipped and frozen in a frame. How discrete
are the bearers, to pantomime real weight
to their burden. So light it takes so many

to lift it down the aisle. So small
I think we've swallowed it—isn't this it
lodged in our throats? At the church door
we take our turns. The mother's still-swollen
belly lurches against us, a great bell silenced.

What went wrong she least of all can tell.
What went wrong was carried beyond telling,
a curl in the surface, a smudge.
A flash flood rips up the shore
and leaves us teetering at the falls.

She knows what we're doing. Running backwards,
reversing the film so this time your face
floats up, your eyes open—the splash unfolding
about you like a full-blown rose—and once again
you're falling through the months toward us.

## Chalk Lineament

He shows up for Easter dinner already
skating against chairs, with the bit
of supermarket sherry he says he brought
for the table. Frayed cuffs, worn shoes
under meticulous polish, ruined gentleman
who is our father. Because it's spring, perhaps,
the sun pouring cordials through the branches,
or because the aroma of the crown roast

my sisters and I shut in the oven
makes him gracious (he's had nothing to eat
since, since . . .), his four-year-old granddaughter
can coax him into her game. In his darned dark suit,
he lies down, spread-eagle on the driveway
among the sloppy five-pointed stars, the outlines
the others left in their turn, and he allows her
to draw the chalk along his body,

her biggest project yet. Along the shoulders,
rounding the shoes with their bumpy laces,
up the slope of the opened leg, the troublesome
baggy crotch—she ends where she began,
the profile he turns to the blacktop to oblige her.
But afterwards he doesn't rise up
from this brief death, and go about his business.
The tar, warm against his back, the serious

small fingers tracing him are luxuries
that soothe him to sleep. When we've laid out
the platters and go to call them, she's dropped
candies into his hands and pockets, polished
stones he pays no mind to. He's intent
on filling the pose, the chalked continent,
having found himself in the suburbs,
inhabiting his own ghost at last.

# Cold Harbor

The traffic pulls its sleeves across the lake
of sleep that inches toward me then rolls away
like mercury. The moon is shrunk
to a china chip in the trees, baffled
by the falling sky. Nights like this the day
won't leave me alone. The wheels
of a grapefruit sliced for breakfast bob up
somehow with the student who wept in my office
embarrassed, patting her wet face
with the report of her blood work
while I dabbed her shoulder and fumbled around.
And what about these crickets? One under our bed now.
Are they nesting in the floorboards? We've found
the knuckle-sized singers on book-spines,
along the ceiling, behind the doorjambs,
creaking through the house until we think
the woods will drown us all.

And tonight in the day's arbitrary flotsam
a black man piling onto a wooden stretcher
gray rags and bones, the Union dead at Cold Harbor.
A picture in a book of pictures, the glossy
guide to the traveling exhibit
we couldn't travel to. I don't think
this man has slept all week either.
His face is shining in the heat, the gray field
shining back at him. I can't see
a tree for miles, a cup of shade
where he might talk low with the others,
shirts and spades that blur
behind the grim stack where he poses.
No trees.
I almost want to wake you up.

Weren't the trees several stories high
that spring we visited the battlefield?
How could they have grown so fast?

In the time it takes to drive the length of this town
from the Quickstop to the tobacco warehouse,
in the time it takes to wash the fixative
over a collodion print,
five acres of Virginia fields went blue
with fallen Union soldiers, a loud
twitching sea, 7,000. Those still alive
in the crossfire scratched out trenches
with bayonet and tin cup and spoon.
The luckiest had friends who dragged them back,
dribbled water across their lips,
and wrote home for them afterwards.
They'd expected the worst. The night before,
they'd sewn inside their collars
scraps of paper with their names and regiments.
The unlucky lay where they dropped. Three days
of moaning, then the long quiet under the sun.
October fogged the fogged faces.
December shagged the timothy and seedlings.

After a week the survivors limped toward Petersburg
where my father's Confederate grandfather
was shot in the siege. And now this burial detail
of former slaves has been sent to do the work
the white men left undone.
All week they've gathered and dug.
Only one government issue boot is in any shape
to walk away. A balustrade
of ribs has collapsed inside a uniform.
The long ulna of an infantryman was dragged out
of its sleeve by crows or dogs.

I wish we'd kept driving that day,
following the muddy roads
until we found the family plot
with my great-grandfather's name chipped
in dark granite perhaps, his relations posted
around him like tent stakes. Winking
behind split levels and furniture outlets,
the Chickahominy steered us into the woods
of the battlepark. Standing clear
of the crumbling breastworks,
the only tourists and all that quiet,
we spun the maps in our hands,
trying to make sense of the battlelines,
to picture so many dead so fast.

If I lie here long enough with the night's
last traffic brushing against the bed,
the crickets slowing to a throb,
will this man pull that knitted cap
from his head, wipe his face
and take up his shovel again? How does he reckon
the moons of calluses on his hands,
the clink of metal on bone?
The war is over, he's free, so he's heard.
How much can the golden scales rise
when he shovels the last mound, taps it down,
and brushes off his hands?
And when he goes on down the road,
a cornucopia curling through palmettos,
how much must he take with him?

We're no one he'd bother to imagine.
The face he lifts to the white photographer

is as blank as he can make it.
We stood quiet in the quiet shade,
but we weren't quiet enough
to hear what he hears, blood drawn
into the spindly roots, into the saplings,
into the crowns above our heads,
and how the day comes on regardless.

# Holler

These are my woods if only because
I've never met a soul in here—
place without a landscape,

this leafy V affords no panorama,
no more view than from a drained
cistern. Look up, the woods

on all sides climb straight up
then open to 30° of sky,
about as far as eyelids open.

A bird whistle in my head,
a brown cricket sentence:
No one ever lived here

and left behind flint or furrow, only
at the trail mouth—as if venturing
further in is too scary

or tiresome—are marks of people,
forlorn parties: beer cans,
a knifed stump, a sock.

I scrambled in over a rickrack
of trees fallen across the dry creek
I tried to walk when the trail

trailed off. Jeans and boots
scraping off chunks of bark
big as book covers, I hoisted myself

over mossy beams that lay waist-
shoulder- neck-high
and overhead—the tide gone out

on a broken-down dock.
A light breeze and now
from high in the canopy,

leaves drift down, indifferent.
Beech, hickory, oak, dull
sycamore spangle together

for a time. Frost has bronzed
a broad bed of ferns, tomorrow
they'll shrivel into threads.

Like all oceans it's an ocean
of time in here. This far in
you'd expect something to happen,

but nothing ever happened here,
ever and ever, sediment,
erasure, this year's leaves

obliterating last. Here are stories
but no plots. I dip my hand in,
brown confetti, and, deeper,

black sponge that tells me
whatever it is I'm looking for,
I won't find it here.

III

# Likeness

*"Ardent imagination, passion, desire—frequently deceived—
produce the figurative style. We do not admit it into history,
for too many metaphors are hurtful . . . to truth, by
saying more or less than the thing itself."*
——*Voltaire,* Philosophical Dictionary

*"midway between the unintelligible and the commonplace,
it is metaphor which produces most knowledge"*
——*Aristotle,* Rhetoric

## 1. EXTREME UNCTION

When Voltaire complained about the church
fathers making history with metaphor
he was complaining about the likes of me
bringing sunlight into it, tiny keys
that spangle the prisoner in his cell
or Christ sliding across the water
like a braking pelican . . .

But in his last hours what figures
played out in his head, what thin similes
that he called for the curate?
Outside the loose splash of a fountain
was too finite to bear, the leaf
sputter on the windowsill a word
too slight for ink and quill?
If you live for Truth, what's a little
unleavened bread, to hedge your bets?

And I can almost imagine it, admitting
at the end the well-groomed priest
to my bedside. He draws the damp sheet back
and oils my feet and hands, sprinkles me
like a shirt for ironing. But just the thought

51

of the host's papery taste revives
a thousand school day masses—the radiators
wheezing beneath the stations of the cross,
the nuns clicking us into genuflection:
IamnotworthyIamnotworthyIam notworthy—

and metaphor lifts the shirt off the ironing board
and floats it through the window.
It folds its arms across its chest
and slips like a letter
into the slot between power lines,
flaps into the sky like the flag
of the spirit (never the spirit itself)
admitting some great reckoner
and shrinks and shrinks to a grain of salt.

Distilled from a test tube, they'd look
the same: blood salt, a dropper
of salt marsh, tears licked up secretly
by the hostage ("I'm still alive then")
or my two-year-old daughter ("I taste me").

## 2. IN THE STAIRWELL

I don't mean a basket of canaries sailed
by paper butterflies. And even the mundane
pickup truck has a *bed*
to carry kindling. Metaphor hitches the impossible
to the passable, the wonder
to the wanderer, tenor and vehicle.
The sun is a clarion and the wind in the cedars
angels choiring in our ears.

After the Christmas concert
I pulled at my friend Rosemarie's sleeve,
"I saw you. What was a good Marxist
like you doing singing along?"
And she smiling back, "And you, a good
atheist, all the words came back to you?"

## 3. THE GOLDEN LEGEND

Like all Catholic kids I prepared myself
early for martyrdom. I chanted the beatific
No's that St. Catherine broke the wheel with,
practiced the stubbornness of St. Denys
on Montmartre, denying his own death, refusing
to fall down where he was killed.
He picked up his severed head, rinsed it off
in a spring and carried it four miles
to the mountain he'd chosen
as his dropping place.
                                    In the garage
I would cut Rainbow bread with a milk glass,
flatten the moons into dry doubloons
that I dropped into my shirt
so my brothers, backyard Romans,
might shower me with the arrows we stripped
from the honeysuckle bush.

                                    The best part was lying
with the cool mud against my back, blooming
like St. Sebastian (a bouquet of branches
shooting from each armpit) and never renouncing
though the soldiers poked me, their aluminum
helmets rattling on their heads like seed pods,
and the clouds made light of it all, inscrutable
grins that broke apart like toast and sped away.

So when I stopped believing I didn't stop
admiring willfulness, great renunciations
that quench pyres, snap ax handles,
and change smuggled bread to roses.
Sunlight rains down keys so tiny they fit

in the tear duct, the fine spray sent up
as Jesus skids toward us like a pelican,
the bucket-beaked fisher of fish
that the old ones believed fed its young
by dripping its own blood down their throats.

It took crates of carrots and steady brushing
by strong-armed grooms to bring out
this lustre in the horses' coats. The gray knot
of cavalry and the lords sporting
Renaissance plumes do not dismount.
This is foot soldier work. The work of halberd
and pike loose in ancient Judea, snow
on every rooftop. The anachronisms
remind us how little of history
is ever reeled in and put away. What happened

twines around *now* and *next*, a knot
in the garden hose that hisses and thrashes
across the lawn. None of these villagers
will shut this day up. They'll carry it
around like a wad of string
in their pockets, something to pick
and pick at: I forgive you nothing.
In the center of the canvas a woman
has sunk to the trampled snow, snow trampled
by hoof and boot. The peasants—their children
scooped up in their arms—are pursued
even into the picture frame. De kindermoord.
In Flemish the massacre sounds like kindling
snapping or small bones. There's no help

from above either—the sky is the same
squalid color as the snow, the yellow
residue of a grease fire. Her child's small
clothes stripped off and tossed beside her,
lost to the world, the woman rocks herself

above the appalling weight they've flung back
in her lap. Pale and pocked as a daylight moon.

Meanwhile, he's out of the picture,
the baby they were after. We will recognize him
in another gallery by the gold plate
fixed to his head. Smuggled south
where spring has already feathered out
the olive and the almond trees, he sucks
the meat of a peeled purple fig
held out in his mother's damp palm.

## 5. EXPERIENCE

After his son died Emerson wandered
his essays trying to feel something again,
hoping that suffering might be it,
the nubbin of truth
that wouldn't melt on the tongue, but:
"The only thing grief has taught me
is to know how shallow it is." A puddle,
a pond, a creek, a wide oblivious river,
sooner or later you hit bottom.

What's the use of metaphor if it can't make loss
fathomable, and the loss of loss:
a fathom is the measure of the arms
outstretched. How to fathom
the child he would never hold again.

And what's the use of history if it can't
make us a bridge to watch the muddle
of what happened ravel towards us, braids slipping
around the pilings that lift us
from the drink and rush
of stuff that hurries under and onward
into what will happen next,
and next. Progress, the love of progress,
and the love of Now We're Getting Somewhere.

We count up what we've learned—
the gouged shore, driftwood
dammed in the rapids, the slow eddies
further back, but the anodyne river
flows into the lake of sleep

and those who know history are
as doomed as anyone else
wading in the understory.
History is no good for figuring somebody
simply walking home one March
from a dawn tennis match.
The desert air cools the sweat
on his neck, and, let's say,
he can make out the smell of the sea
woven inside the smell of coffee and snow
sloughing off the peak of Qurnet es Sauda.
A dark Mercedes rounds the corner
and that's the last he sees of history
for seven years: "I have become a bandied name
that floats in a white place, cramped
and smooth, like a sparrow egg."

Here comes the flotsam of the flooded house:
stair parts, highchair, Christmas cards,
low boat of a locked bureau. Upstream
keys and silverware fall through clouds
of minnows and sink into the mud.

## 6. TOUR FROM THE CELL

"Duck your head here where the stairway
curls us into the blue that day begins with,
now step onto the sunsoaked street
(feel the hair on your arms rising, the heat
under your shoes). Cover your eyes a moment.
Do you smell garlic and cardamom
and raisins? Coffee? That luffing sound
is rice poured in a basket, polished

infinitesimal pearls. Behind the jalousie
my wife braids her hair. On her long brown
fingers let's give her amethysts set in silver.
The saffron taxis wait for us. Let's circle
the fountain in the plaza, twirling our keys
and blowing smoke rings at the clouds."

## 7. AFTER AUDEN

Rocking on his heels, reading the literature,
smoking, the young poet ("tall, with straw-
yellow hair and light hazel eyes")
stood where we stood in Room 31. Another December,
"the cold streets tangled like old string,"
1938. That month after Kristallnacht
you could feel what was coming, the cobblestones
throbbing under your feet, the click
of bolts in locks, shudders. Children
forbidden to go skating peek out,
but only a bit of tank, a wheel, the chin
of an officer fits in the keyhole.
Wheels rattling stone and the sound of gorgeous
creaking leather, the butter of their boots.

For an hour we slumped in the ancient chaise,
the velvet nap balding under our arms,
and joked how *Icarus*—smaller, duller
than we'd supposed—had shrunk and faded
from too much washing in poetry.
Among the distant gliding sea birds,
cormorants and pelicans? (curve of wing
fine as eyelashes above the headlands)
we searched for the father who by now
would have glanced over his shoulder
and doubled back, opening and closing
his winged arms around the updrafts
before the fathoms blinked over his child
and slapped against the delicate ship.

And I remembered Bishop writing Lowell
that about suffering Auden was wrong:

"the ploughman and the people on the boat
will rush to see the falling boy any minute,
they always do, though maybe not to help."
The eastbound traffic slows and snarls
to count the westbound sirens, look long
at the skid marks, the crushed car, an arm
dangling from a stretcher. And the shepherds
would soonest tramp down the hillside
for the miraculous birth of a two-headed calf.

## 8. GRAVENSTEEN

Back home I'd been following the story
like bread crumbs into the woods—news flash,
special report. The pale men appeared
one by one, first in Damascus in a flashbulb
storm, then on the balcony at Wiesbaden,
another white bath of attention.
I didn't much believe all the talk
of global village, electronic Earth,
but there I was in Ghent, in that strange orange
rhombus of a Eurostyle room,
glued to CNN updates, like people
in Paducah and Palermo, waiting for the last
US hostage, Terry Anderson, to step
onto the hospital balcony. Seven years
out of history: he looked intact
except his wirerims were missing a temple piece.

But I had a duty to sightsee, so while my husband
gave his paper at the university,
I forced myself into the Christmas crowds
along the Veldstraat, buttoned my Blue Guide deep
in my pockets to disguise myself, and strode
toward Gravensteen, the reconstructed Castle
of the Counts, a gray pile in the frozen river Lief.

Off season, I was the only person nosing
around the dim chamber, my breath misting
the display cases, not that I could read
the Flemish placards anyway. Double doors
for a dollhouse?—some arched devices
that met at screws, tiny padlocks dangling

like earrings from one side.
Whatever was laid out under glass,
I thought I knew enough to appreciate
the fortitude of craft. Though the blacksmith
had long ago sunk to dust and chalk,
what glowed once on his anvil, what he forged
in the white heat and clang, iron on iron,
was unchanged, a legacy to drift
toward us through the centuries.

I made out a long cot in a corner,
wrought iron letters on poles, cleavers,
chains and bracelets: what was this place?
I picked out a few English cognates—
finger, justice, state prisoner—
and found I'd been admiring
thumbscrew, branding iron, "coercive bed"
in The Museum of Judicial Objects.

What was I so suddenly afraid of?
Hospital-hospitality-hostage-host:
like the knowledge of good and evil
our words are tangled up, our little
victories over oblivion. The great cloth hall
is black with soot. The bolts of silk
the merchants wrangled over
were soon ragged, then lint, then less
than dust—seedlings for clouds, the speck
you can't find in your tearing eye.
The figures on Penelope's tapestry,
the thread, and then the loom.
What's left is our metalwork—the iron age,
the bronze age, the ages of spearhead,
arrowhead, manacle and the executioner's sword
—as unchanged as we are.

## 9. LIKENESS

A crookneck squash, a skeleton key,
the chevron penciling
of a flown bird, these are all "horse"
to our daughter. And the moon
that says O O between the trees sleeps
on the kitchen table, escorted
by fork and spoon. As it came to each of us,
language comes to her first in resemblance
shimmering between things, trailing
clouds of glory and metaphor.
But the double-eyed happenstance
in our "moon" doesn't make it moonier
than the sidelong glance in "maand"
or the cup in "luna."

With the kindling shed by the silver
maple I spell out HORSE for her.
Horse, I say, and she plops on the H's
crosspiece and rides it into slivers.
But when we park the car, jump the ditch
and wade thistle and stinkweed
to a pasture fence, Anna freezes against me,
clinging to my legs as the chestnut mare—
a sudden brown ocean of glistening flesh—
snorts the grass from my hands,
grinds it between large yellow teeth, then reaches
its neck through the barbwire for more.

# Flesh Is Air Too

*"Dead, but still with us, still with us but dead."*
*"Having it both ways is a thing I like."*
                    —Donald Barthelme

Along a canal I glance in a dim doorway
and stop stunned. That suede jacket, that urbane gaze,
that whimsy of a beard—materialized
at a table is Don Barthelme, a goblet of wine
like a ball of amber in his hand.
Five years dead but here he is in Amsterdam.

All yesterday the sleeves of air
were blown inside out. I had to laugh
to keep my footing against a wind that lifted
everything loose and loosened everything fast.
The promenading trees tossed
ladder rungs at my toes
like celestial anagrams. Beside bridges dogs groped
for leashes and cats in windows griped
about their fur rubbed
the right way. The gale regaled us.
Body without mass, mass
without body: the contract dreamed between land
and air broken. And now as if a patch of tall grass
were blown back to reveal some long lost
watch stem or fountain pen, here is Don,
hiding in the open like a palindrome.

When he sees I recognize him,
he gives me a nod, raises a finger
to his lips: shhh. Don't tell them
where I am, or that I am?
Or Keep quiet and watch? Then
I notice the tables around him—at each one

sits a man or woman, a flickering person
who stops like a candle flame when a door is shut.

Their clothes give them away, hobnailed shoes,
mackinaws, felt hats, the women's hose
rolled down to their ankles.
I start to ask him Why me? but they turn genial
faces to me, smiling like people
glad to be found out: that I happened to see
is as immaterial as they are. Smoothly
as soap bubbles blown through hoops,
each figure projects itself in quadruplicate
around each table, a bridge party
of mirrors, a display of how they can tarry
or go as they please. Their bodies
free, they're free as words to be everywhere at once

—in the small hours the empty pubs of Dublin
and Canberra, the taqueria of Houston,
the grassy crossroads of Guinea, the stalls
of Delhi, Marakesh, and Tanzania are full
of the convivial dead. Then the immaterial
is hereafter, one world
a ghost rhyme of the next? I think I see Don nod
but I'm wafted back to bed in Amsterdam, a wad
of down settling in dawn's thin doorway.

## A NOTE ON THE AUTHOR

Michelle Boisseau grew up in Cincinnati and was educated at Ohio University (B.A., M.A.) and the University of Houston (Ph.D.). Her first book, *No Private Life* (Vanderbilt University Press), was published in 1990. Her poems have earned her a fellowship from the National Endowment for the Arts and prizes from the Poetry Society of America. She is co-author (with Robert Wallace) of *Writing Poems*, 4th ed. (HarperCollins). She taught at Morehead State University, situated in the Daniel Boone National Forest in Kentucky, before joining the faculty at the University of Missouri–Kansas City in 1995.

## A NOTE ON THE PRIZE

The Samuel French Morse Poetry Prize was established in 1983 by the Northeastern University Department of English in order to honor Professor Morse's distinguished career as teacher, scholar, and poet. The members of the prize committee are Francis C. Blessington, Joseph deRoche, Victor Howes, Ruth Lepson, Stuart Peterfreund, P. Carey Reid, and Guy Rotella.